# BUZZY B

Written by Sally Morgan

## Collins

A bee is small and hairy with six legs and wings. Bees have a sting that can hurt people. They use the sting to stay safe.

hairs

head

wings

sting

legs

Bees make a buzzing sound when they beat their wings up and down.

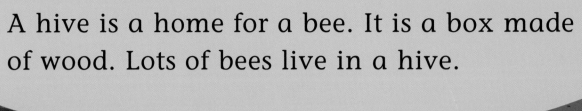

A hive is a home for a bee. It is a box made of wood. Lots of bees live in a hive.

Some bees live in nests in holes in trees and walls.

Bees come out and look for flowers when it is sunny. When it is wet, they stay inside.

The top bee in the hive is the queen. The queen is bigger and longer than the rest of the bees.

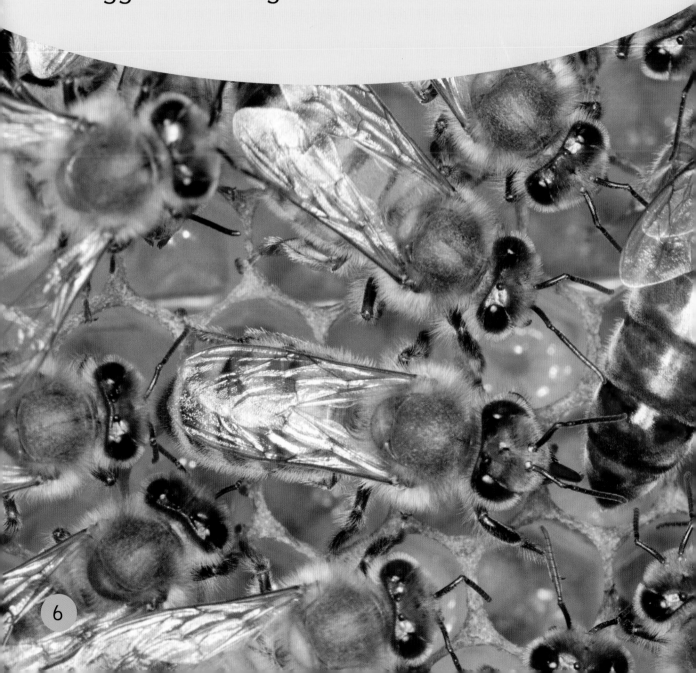

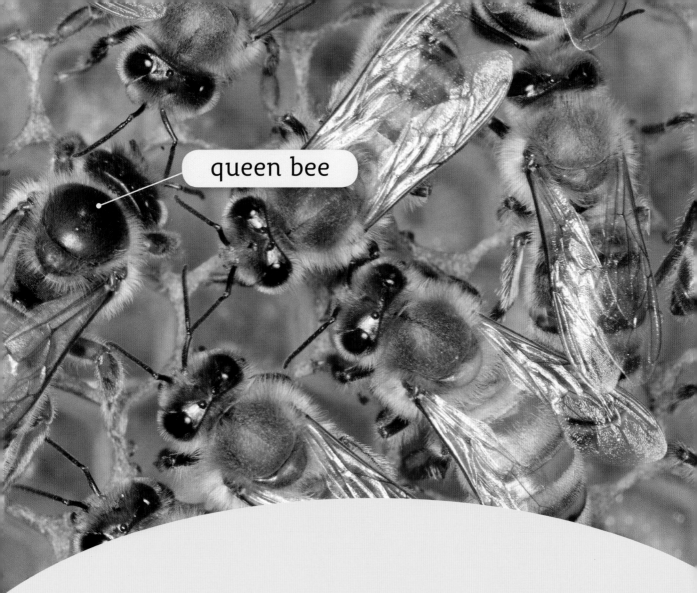

queen bee

There is just one queen and she stays in the hive. All the bees help the queen. They bring her food and care for her.

Bees fly from flower to flower to look for nectar. Nectar is a food. It is found inside the flower.

Bees sip the sweet nectar in the flower. As they do this, they pick up yellow dust. This is pollen.

nectar

pollen

They take the nectar and pollen back to the hive.

Bees make nectar and pollen into food.
They keep their food in the hive to eat.
They eat a lot of food in winter.

bees eating

wax walls

In the hive bees make wax. They chew the wax and make it into walls in the hive. This keeps the food safe.

Flowers need bees. As bees fly from flower to flower they leave a bit of pollen and new flowers grow.

pollen

It is good that we have bees to help flowers
and food to grow.

# Bees

flowers

nectar

hive

pollen

food

bee

wax

15

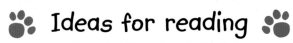

# Ideas for reading

Written by Clare Dowdall, PhD
*Lecturer and Primary Literacy Consultant*

**Learning objectives:** apply phonic knowledge and skills as the prime approach to reading and spelling unfamiliar words; identify the constituent parts of two-syllable and three-syllable words to support the application of phonic knowledge and skills; read phonically decodable two-syllable and three-syllable words; find specific information in simple texts; experiment with and build new stores of words to communicate in different texts

**Curriculum links:** Science

**Focus phonemes:** zz, qu, ee, ea, ar, ur, ow, a-e, i-e, u-e

**Fast words:** their, they, one, when, there

**Word count:** 277

## Getting started

- Fast read words containing *qu* and *zz* using word cards, e.g. buzz, buzzy, jazz, jazzy, fizz, fizzy, quiz, queen, quick.

- Explain that the letter *q* always needs a *u* to follow it. Help children to make simple *qu* words using magnetic letters.

- Look at the front cover. Explain that this is an information book. Read the title and ask children to describe what they can see. Discuss why bees are described as *buzzy*.

- Read the blurb together. Remind children of strategies for reading longer words, e.g. looking for smaller known units within words like *fl-ow-ers*, to increase the speed of reading.

- Ask children to suggest what the food is and what is happening in the illustration on the back cover. Continue to introduce new vocabulary, and build a word list for children to use.

## Reading and responding

- Discuss what children know about bees and make a list of questions to prepare them for reading and finding out.